ATTACHMENT THEORY WORKBOOK

Why is your attachment type impacting upon your happiness in relationships? Discover how to identify who is right for you and help to heal your wounds

DAVID LAWSON PHD

TABLE OF CONTENTS

INTRODUCTION

Whether we are aware of it or not, the experiences of our childhood play an enormous role in determining the people we are today. The relationships we had as children with our parents, or other primary caregivers have a profound effect on the way we react to situations in our lives, and the way we interact with the people around us.

As young children, we respond instinctively to the kind of love and support offered to us by our parents or carers. While a strong bond to our primary caregiver is critical for our development in these early years, difficulties arising from this attachment can lead to problems with relationships and self-image in later life.

Extensive scientific research has proven that everyone has a certain "love style" or manner of behavior within relationships, based on their experiences as a young child. For example, children who grow up with strict, disciplinary parents often learn early to bury their emotions out of fear of being reprimanded. This trait often continues long into adulthood, with such people finding it hard to share their feelings and connect with others. Those who grow up with unpredictable or inconsistent parenting with often seek attention through raising their voice or expressing anger and frustration in other ways. Their self-image is, as a result, less than positive. Conversely, children who grow up feeling a secure and loving attachment to their primary caregiver usually become trusting adults with a positive self-image.

Of course, these behaviors are often unconscious and instinctive, making them difficult to recognize. These unidentified behaviors can cause us to have problems as adults when it comes to making friends, finding love and developing meaningful relationships.

Think back to the environment you grew up in. Was your relationship with your parents or caregivers a healthy and secure one, or did you recognize a little of yourself in any of the above situations? Perhaps you have never thought to examine the way your upbringing is affecting you today.

But if you have identified with any of these issues, all is not lost. The patterns and beliefs we develop as children, though often deeply ingrained in our psyche, can be unlearned and replaced with more helpful beliefs and approaches to life.

In this book, you will discover the specific ways in which our childhood attachment experiences shape and affect our adult experience, along with proven methods for reducing their effect and eliminating your own troublesome behavior in many areas of your life.

Are you unable to maintain a successful romantic relationship? Do you see the same patterns emerging in your relationships with partner after partner? Perhaps you have questioned what you are doing wrong, or why you always seem to attract the same kind of person, who will treat you in the same negative way. Or maybe you are aware that you yourself are the problem. Perhaps you have found yourself repeatedly sabotaging your relationships and turning people away. Do you see the same behavior in yourself again and again, but are unable to make changes? If this sounds like you, it may be time to examine this behavior and the way your romantic relationships are affected by your childhood experiences of attachment.

In order to do this, we will examine the four attachment styles of love, and the way attachment affects your ability to interact with your significant other. Understand your love style and conversely, the *way* you love, will assist you in recognizing – and putting an end to – any destructive behavior. By identifying your instinctive behavior, you will be able to anticipate your reaction to specific situations and alter your behavior accordingly. Understanding your love style will help you form the healthy and fulfilling romantic relationship you have been waiting for.

Of course, it is not necessary to have a life partner in order to be happy. Our attachment style has as profound an effect on our relationship with ourselves as it does on our relationship with others. Addressing the ways our self-worth and self-image is affected by our past relationships is crucial to finding lasting happiness. This book will address these issues, along with the many ways of feeling good about yourself and your life when going it alone, whether you have chosen to be single, or are yet to find the one you have been searching for.

Perhaps you have found your behavioral patterns resurfacing when interacting with people other than your romantic partner. Our attachment styles come into play in many other relationships too, such as with close friends, colleagues, family and even strangers. We will examine how personal attachment can affect your relationships in many different facets and will look at ways to adapt your behavior accordingly. This can help you build lasting friendships, productive working relationships and a strong support network.

Finally, we will take an extensive look at attachment wounds and examine proven ways to heal them, resulting in stronger and healthier relationships in all facets of life.

By implementing the strategies presented in this book, you will be able to identify, address and remove harmful beliefs and behavioral patterns you have likely carried around since childhood. Though removing these deeply ingrained beliefs is no easy task, it is an extremely worthwhile investment of your time and energy. By healing attachment wounds and replacing learned negative behavior with more positive traits, you will see marked improvements in your relationship with both yourself and others.

So are you ready to release negative behavior caused by your attachment and love styles once and for all? Are you ready to embrace a healthier, happier life full of rewarding relationships?

Let's get started.

CHAPTER ONE: HOW OUR CHILDHOOD AFFECTS US IN LATER LIFE

E arly childhood is a time of discovery. Everything around us is new, and each day is full of exploration and learning. It the time that we begin to make sense of the complex world around us.

As children, we absorb information at a particularly rapid rate. At a young age, it is far easier to learn a foreign language, or to play music by ear, for example, as we are so open to taking in new information. But as children, we also absorb beliefs and patterns of behavior that come about as a result of those around us.

Primarily, our beliefs and behaviors are shaped by our connection to our primary caregivers – in most cases, our parents. Our relationship with our mother and father can instill patterns of behavior deep within us that can affect us all through our lives. These behavioral patterns can be either positive or negative.

The concept of attachment theory was introduced by British psychologist John Bowlby in the 1950s and 60s. To formulate the theory, Bowlby sought information from a variety of fields such as biology, developmental psychology, cognitive science and evolution to understand the mechanisms behind a child's ties to its mother.

Secure Attachment

As children, we learn ways of responding to those around us, along with methods of coping and reacting to the situations we find ourselves in. When we are offered love, support, and attention, we will respond positively, forming a *secure* attachment style.

As young children, our instinct is to examine and explore the world around us, in order to make discoveries about ourselves, our bodies and the environment we live in. Research has proven that a secure bond to our primary caregiver is crucial for our development. When we have a secure, loving connection to this caregiver, we feel safe going out into the world to explore, knowing that Mom or Dad will always be there to keep us safe. Our primary caregiver becomes our safe haven; someone to whom we can always return to and find comfort.

Having a secure connection with our primary caregiver usually leads to children becoming trusting adults who have no difficulty connecting to others and forming meaningful relationships. If a child feels secure at the age of one or two, they will go on to make friends at kindergarten, then at school, all the way through to college and work. They are optimistic, with a positive self-image. Most children with a secure attachment style go on to have successful adult lives, including happy marriages, strong relationship with their children and a large income.

Insecure Attachment

But not everyone is lucky enough to have had a strong and loving relationship with their parents. What about those among us who struggled for attention from distant, overworked parents? Or, worse, those who grew up with a caregiver who was physically or emotionally abusive? Sadly, these situations are anything but rare. Let's take a look at how these situations affect us, both as children, and in later life.

If our bond with our caregiver is weak, the thought of venturing out into the world can seem frightening. We do not have the trust that we will have a safe place to return to when our adventures are over, and nor do we trust that Mom or Dad will always be there to protect us. If we are insecurely attached to our primary caregiver as a child, it can lead to trust issues as an adult, along with a lack of social skills and problems forming meaningful relationships. Insecurely attached children often struggle to make friends at an early age, a pattern which can continue throughout their life.

There are three types of insecure attachment styles that can affect us throughout our life. Let's take a look at the causes and characteristics of each:

Anxious Ambivalent Attachment

Let's say we grow up with a single mom who works long hours to make ends meet. While this mom may be loving, as children we focus on the fact that she is not always there for us. We view the relationship as inconsistent and insecure. As a result, we can become clingy, needing to take advantage of our mother's attention when we feel lucky enough to have it. But Mom always has work to do, and even though she might have the best of intentions, she is not able to give us attention as much as we would like.

We come to believe the only way to get her attention is to raise our emotional state, by screaming and throwing tantrums. And when we finally receive that predictable, loving response from Mom we have been seeking, we act ambivalent and detached, disguising our true feelings.

Children who have an anxious ambivalent attachment style often grow up to be unpredictable, moody adults. They struggle with self-esteem issues and often have a less-than-positive image of themselves.

Anxious Avoidant Attachment

Now let's imagine we grow up in a home in which our primary caregiver is a strict father. Dad loves us and wants the best for us, but he believes – perhaps due to his own upbringing – that heavy discipline is the best way to raise a strong and resilient child. When we get too loud, or express to much emotion, Dad gets angry and punishes us. As Dad is frightening when he is angry, we quickly learn not to show our emotions, in order to avoid antagonizing him.

We come to believe that showing our feelings equates to punishment and, consequently, fear. We quickly learn that it is best to keep our feelings hidden deep inside – both in front of Dad and in other situations, such as in the classroom, or among friends. We see this as a way of protecting ourselves from harm.

Children who have an anxious avoidant attachment style will often carry this same belief throughout their life. They find it difficult to express their feelings and often have trouble forming meaningful relationships. This leads to a negative self-view and lack of self-worth.

Anxious Disorganised Attachment

This attachment style differs from the other two insecure attachment styles (and the single secure attachment style) by acting in a chaotic, disorganised manner when faced with distress.

Let's say we grow up with parents who are distant and self-absorbed. Sometimes they may even be physically abusive. When placed in such a situation as a child, we become anxious to be around the people we rely on for security and care. This inner conflict completely disorganizes our beliefs about love, safety and security. Being in such an environment causes us to feel fear, without any resolution (in the form of a show of love). In response, we seek to avoid all social situations and contact with others. We see this as a way of protecting ourselves from harm. We become withdrawn and are starved of love.

Children with an anxious avoidant attachment style often grow up believing themselves unworthy of love. This, in turn, affects their ability to form relationships, and express themselves effectively. Their self-worth, as a result, is usually extremely low.

Toxic Stress

Our attachment style is formed in the very first years of life, at a time in which we are too young to communicate our anxiety effectively. As a result of this struggle to convey our concerns, we can experience high levels of stress. This stress activates the fight or flight response, which causes our adrenal glands to produce the stress hormones adrenaline and cortisol. Our heart rate and blood pressure increase and we become increasingly alert. When the fight or flight response is engaged frequently, it becomes what is known as ***toxic stress.***

As you are most likely aware, stress is one of the major issues in our busy, modem lives. It can lead to all manner of health issues, from heart disease to cancer and everything in between. But toxic stress can have an even more severe effect on children. Increased levels of adrenalin and cortisol can impair a child's brain development and weakens their immune system. Prior to birth, or in the first months of life, toxic stress can go so far as to switch the expressions of our genes, which can cause health problems to appear years, and even decades, later.

The Long-Term Effects of Our Attachment Styles

As you can see from the above examples, our attachment styles have a great effect on us all the way through our lives. But these effects are far from theoretical. In the 1970s, researchers at Minnesota University began a study through which they were able to predict from the age of three whether or not a child would drop out of high school, as based on their attachment style. Their results were proven to have 77% accuracy.

Another study, conducted at Harvard University in the 1950s, asked its undergraduate subjects how close they felt to their parents. Thirty-five years later, these same subjects were surveyed about their health. Ninety-one percent of those who claimed they had a negative or broken relationship with their primary caregiver were suffering from health issues such as heart disease, high blood pressure and alcoholism. Conversely, among subjects with a warm and loving relationship with their parents, only 45% reported suffering from health issues.

*

Although we have the ability, to some degree, to choose who we are and what we want to become, there is no doubt that the experiences of our childhood shape us to an extent. Understanding exactly what our attachment styles are and how they affect us in our experience and perception of the world can go a long way to helping us manage any negative behaviors springing from our attachment style.

CHAPTER TWO: UNDERSTANDING LOVE STYLES – ATTACHMENT STYLES IN ROMANTIC RELATIONSHIPS

As we have learned, there are four distinct style of attachment when it comes to a child's relationship with his or her primary caregiver. Our childhood attachment style can have far-reaching implications on the way we react to situations in later life.

One of the greatest facets of life affected by our childhood attachment styles is our ability to love and build romantic relationships.

Perhaps this is what drew you to this book. Maybe you always seem to attract partners with similar characteristic. Or perhaps you continually date people who don't turn out to be as compatible with you as you first thought.

But have you ever stopped to think about why you are attracted to the people you are?

Falling in love and building relationships involves constant choice, commitment and work. While love can be extremely rewarding, and even exhilarating, it is often far from easy. Connecting with a romantic partner requires us to develop an understanding of the behavior of both our loved one and ourselves.

Researchers have determined that everyone has a certain *love style*, based on their upbringing. A love style is constituted of our behaviors and inclinations with regards to how we respond to our romantic partners. By making sense of the way we love, we can learn how our love styles affect our relationships. Understanding our inclinations and tendencies in relationships can help us to make sense of our own – and our partner's –behaviour, and build stronger, long-lasting relationships.

The four attachment styles of love are closely linked to the childhood attachment styles discussed in the previous chapter. Let's take a closer look:

Secure Love Style

Those of us lucky enough to have a secure love attachment style have a significant advantage when it comes to finding partners and maintaining meaningful, loving relationships. People with a secure love style generally feel able to go to their partner with any issues or problems, allowing for meaningful, productive discussions. A secure love style also means you have great trust in your partner, allowing them the freedom to explore their own interests and pursue their own goals.

This leads to open, loving and honest relationships in which both partners are equal. It provides an environment in which both parties can thrive, grow and be happy.

Having a secure love style means we are comfortable having separate interests from our lover, but also understanding how to mesh and work together to build a loving and secure partnership with which to go through life.

Maybe you're thinking this all sounds too good to be true. But it's important not to confuse a secure love style with perfection. Because, as we know, perfection is something unattainable, especially when it comes to love and relationships.

Having a secure attachment style does not mean we are immune from conflict, arguments and bad days. Far from it. The nature of building a romantic relationship means there will always be disagreements. But where those with a secure attachment style differ is in their ability to work with their partner to problem solve, in order to reach an agreeable resolution to any conflict that may arise. Those with a secure attachment style also have a higher emotional intelligence, which leads them to seek solutions, rather than acting rashly, striking out or attacking their loved one.

Great resilience and self-awareness are typical characteristics of people with a secure love style – traits that assist them in moving past obstacles and conflicts in a mature and loving way. Secures have the capacity to reflect on their own emotional states, along with the emotional states of their partner. This allows them to communicate more effectively. As a result, secures perform well in partnerships and are able to respond appropriately to the emotional messages they are sent by their loved one.

Outside of romantic relationships, people with a secure attachment style make excellent colleagues, due to their ability to work well in teams. On average, they have higher incomes than those with insecure attachment styles.

Though we will look more closely at ways of assessing attachment style in the following chapter, if you can answer yes to most or all of these questions, you may exhibit a secure attachment style:

- Do you feel a strong emotional connection to the loved ones in your life?
- Are you comfortable with emotional and physical closeness?
- Are you equally comfortable with independence?
- Do you feel as though you communicate effectively?
- Do you have the ability to resolve conflicts when they arise?
- Do you feel as though the relationships in your life are fairly stable?
- Do you trust your partner?
- Do you feel comfortable opening up and being vulnerable around your partner?

Anxious Preoccupied Love Style

For people with an anxious preoccupied love style, love is often a thing relegated to the world of fantasy. They romanticize love, and are prone to falling for a fantasy, or unobtainable ideal, as this is far easier to manage than the often-challenging reality of maintaining a relationship.

This romantic view of love often leads anxious preoccupied lovers to be attracted to partners who they perceive as "needing saving," or, conversely, partners they believe can save them. Anxious preoccupied lovers often find themselves seeking an unobtainable fairy-tale ending.

People with this attachment style often suffer from insecurities and self-doubt and struggle to find a strong sense of their own identity.

Whilst in a relationship, people with this attachment style can be clingy, demanding and obsessive. They often overthink and overanalyze situations and can be moody and unpredictable. As a result, their relationships can be tempestuous and troubled, with anxious preoccupied lovers mistaking this constant conflict for passion.

Outside of romantic relationships, people with an anxious preoccupied attachment style are often dissatisfied with their jobs and have a lower income than those in a secure relationship.

If you answer yes to some or all of the following questions, you may exhibit and anxious preoccupied love style:

- When you argue with your loved one, does it make you feel extremely anxious and overwhelmed?
- When your partner requests a little alone time, do you hound them for attention until they give in?
- Do you feel the need for constant reassurance within your relationship?
- If your partner is away, does it make you question their love for you?

The anxious preoccupied love style is closely tied to the anxious ambivalent attachment style. Generally, those who exhibit one will also exhibit the other.

Dismissive Avoidant Love Style

A dismissive avoidant love style is characterized by being distant and detached in relationships. People with this attachment style often have strong personalities and come across as independent and self-sufficient.

But this strength is often just a cover for their inability to share feelings and express their emotions. People with this love style often withdraw at the first sign of conflict, cutting themselves off from any chance at true emotional intimacy.

It's important, of course, in any relationship, for both people to have personal space and time away from their partner. But those of us with a dismissive avoidant love style will seek solitude far more often than most people. They will often push their partner away and deflect their advances, seeking the safety of their own personal space. In the eyes of someone with a dismissive avoidant love style, spending time with a romantic partner puts them at risk of being vulnerable and getting hurt.

When crisis hits a relationship, in the form of conflict, or even a breakup, people with this love style have the ability to close themselves off and convince themselves – at least for a while – that they don't care about what's happening. Their strong, independent personality kicks in, and they convince themselves they are happy on their own.

But this steely independence can only last so long. As humans, we need contact with others in order to survive. None of us can prosper on our own. The reality is that the steely façade portrayed by people with a dismissive avoidant love style is just a front for a deep-seated lack of self-worth.

Those with a dismissive avoidant love style will avoid shows of affection such as hugs, and will often avoid making eye contact.

A dismissive avoidant love style can manifest itself outside of romantic relationships too. People with this love style have difficulty maintaining close relationships of all kinds, whether with friends, family or lovers.

The most extreme avoidants are almost entirely incapable of talking about their feelings. The feelings they do have are primarily negative and they have great difficulty putting them into words. This is known as *alexithymia* – a syndrome referring to the inability to find words for feelings. It is important to note that this is not the same as *not having* feelings. Extreme avoidants suffering from alexithymia are often only able to express themselves through rage and tantrums. Their emotions can also manifest as physical symptoms such as unexplained stomach pains or rushes of adrenalin.

Outside of romantic relationships, people with an avoidant attachment style are prone to being workaholics. Letting work take over their life is often a ploy to avoid social situations. Avoidants generally prefer to work alone. Because of their work ethic, their incomes are often as high as those with a secure attachment style, but they are often just as dissatisfied with their jobs as anxious preoccupieds. However, their work ethic and ability to act alone makes people with avoidant personalities excel in roles that require individual effort. Their lack of empathy and concern for others' feelings can also be beneficial in fields such as litigation.

If you can answer yes to some or all of the following questions, you may exhibit a dismissive avoidant attachment style:

- Do you feel closest to your loved ones when you are apart?
- Do you find yourself pulling away when your partner is seeking emotional or physical intimacy?

- Do you seek to remove yourself from stressful situations of conflict?
- Do you feel emotionally disconnected from others?

The dismissive avoidant love style is most often exhibited by people with an anxious avoidant attachment style.

Fearful Avoidant Love Style

For people with a fearful avoidant love style, maintaining a relationship is something of a juggling act. They simultaneously fear being both too close and too distant from their partner. For those with fearful avoidant attachment issues, love can be akin to a terrifying roller-coaster ride.

Such people understand that, in order to build a strong relationship, they must allow themselves to get close to another person. But doing this makes them fearful, as they are scared of being abandoned. They struggle to build trust and rely on their partner, and often have little confidence in the strength of their relationship.

Unsurprisingly, this leads them to behave unpredictably, and they can become overwhelmed by the intensity and inconsistency of their own emotions. People with this attachment style struggle with endless inner conflict: on one hand, they crave intimacy, and on the other, they resist it, out of fear of getting hurt.

For fearful avoidant lovers, relationships are often full of highs and lows. They often find themselves clinging to their partner when they start to feel rejected, which, in some cases, can lead to emotionally and physically abusive relationships.

Just like with the dismissive avoidant love style, these traits can lead a person to have few close friends and meaningful relationships in all facets of their life.

If you can answer yes to any of the following questions, you may exhibit a fearful avoidant attachment style:

- Do you desperate seek emotional intimacy, but simultaneously feel as though it's safer to be on your own?
- Do you feel like emotional or physical intimacy will led to you getting hurt?
- As a child, was your primary caregiver physically or emotionally abusive?
- Did your primary caregiver show love one minute and hurt you the next?

The fearful avoidant love style is most often exhibited by those with an anxious disorganized attachment style.

*

Can you see yourself in any of the above examples?

If it is all still a little hazy, don't panic. In the next chapter, we will look more closely at exactly how to determine your own attachment style, particularly with regards to romantic love.

CHAPTER THREE: WHAT IS YOUR ATTACHMENT STYLE?

We have begun to explore the attachment and love styles, as theorized by a number of prominent psychologists. Perhaps you have already begun to identify some of these characteristics within yourself, your partner, or your children.

No doubt you are also beginning to realize just how beneficial knowing your attachment style can be. For parents, identifying their child's attachment style can assist them in recognizing the challenges their children face on a daily basis, and how their own behaviour may be contributing to their child's issues.

And for those of us seeking to understand how attachment style affects our romantic life, understanding our own and our partner's tendencies and inclinations can go a long way towards anticipating and resolving conflict.

As attachment style is such a key thing to determine, psychologists have developed a number of tests to determine attachment and love styles in both adults and children. Let's take a look at the methods used to ascertain these crucial pieces of information:

Determining Attachment Style in Young Children

Experts believe that our attachment style is formed as early as the age of one. Tests have been developed in order to determine attachment style in babies and young children, in hope that this can help eliminate insecure attachment as soon as possible.

The test involves allowing the child to play with its mother, or primary caregiver, inside a room for several minutes. Then the child is left alone. After several minutes, the mother returns to the room. They key moment is the child's reaction to the return of the mother.

If a child is securely attached, they will usually hug their mother, before quickly calming down and returning to the game they were playing. Children with an insecure attachment style can react in a number of negative ways; from acting ambivalent and avoidant to crying and refusing to continue playing, despite their mother's attempts to soothe them.

Determining Attachment Styles in Adults

But what about determining our own love and attachment styles?

Widely accepted as one of the most meaningful advances in 20th century psychology, a short questionnaire used to determine attachment style was devised by University of Denver psychologists, Phillip Shaver and Cindy Hazan.

The questionnaire first appeared in 1985 in The Rocky Mountain News, a local Colorado newspaper.

The questionnaire provided readers with three simply statements about behaviors in love, and asked them to pick which they felt most closely resembled them. This presented readers with three possible love style options – secure, avoidant or anxious.

So let's go ahead and take Shaver and Hazan's questionnaire:

Which of the following to do you feel most closely resembles you in love?

A. I am somewhat uncomfortable being close to others; I find it difficult to trust them completely, and find it difficult to allow myself to depend on them. I am nervous when anyone gets too close, and often, others want me to be more intimate than I feel comfortable being.

B. I find it relatively easy to get close to others and am comfortable depending on them and having them depend on me. I don't worry about being abandoned or about someone getting too close to me.

C. I find that others are reluctant to get as close to me as I would like. I often worry that my partner doesn't really love me or won't want to stay with me. I want to get very close to my partner, and this sometimes scares people away.

(Note that, in this case, "close" refers to emotional attachment, and may or may not include sexual intimacy.)

As you may have already determined, those selecting choice A are experiencing an ***avoidant*** love attachment style. (Either dismissive avoidant or fearful avoidant) Choice B represents ***secure*** attachment, while choice C indicates an ***anxious preoccupied*** love attachment style.

Over the years, psychologists have built on Hazan and Shaver's initial questionnaire developing further tests to determine attachment styles within adults.

The following quiz is a variation of a study devised by the Fetzer Institute in Michigan, US.

1.	I'm afraid that my partner will stop loving me.	1234567
2.	I often worry that my partner will leave me.	1234567
3.	I often worry that my partner's love for me is not real.	1234567

4.	I worry that I will care about my romantic partners more than they care for me.	1234567
5.	I often find myself wishing that my partner's feelings for me were as strong as my feelings for him or her.	1234567
6.	I am constantly worrying about the security of my relationships.	1234567
7.	When my partner and I are apart, I worry that he or she might become interested in someone else.	1234567
8.	When I show my feelings for romantic partners, I get nervous that they will reject me, or will not feel the same about me.	1234567
9.	I often worry about my partner leaving me.	1234567
10.	My romantic partner sometimes makes me doubt myself.	1234567
11.	I can't help worrying about being abandoned.	1234567
12.	I feel like my romantic partners never get as close to me as I would like them to.	1234567

13.	Sometimes my romantic partners seem to change their feelings about me for no apparent reason.	1234567
14.	My need for physical and emotional intimacy often scares people away.	1234567
15.	I'm afraid that once my partner gets to who I really am, he or she won't like me.	1234567
16.	I get made when I do not get the support and affection I need from my partner.	1234567
17.	I constantly worry that I am not good enough for other people.	1234567
18.	My partner only seems to notice I'm around when I get angry.	1234567
19.	I feel uncomfortable showing my partner how I really feel.	1234567
20.	I don't like sharing my private thoughts and feelings with my partner.	1234567

21.	I don't allow myself to depend on my romantic partners.	1234567
22.	I do not feel very comfortable being close to my romantic partners.	1234567
23.	I don't feel comfortable opening up and sharing with my partners.	1234567
24.	I prefer not to get too close – emotionally or physically – with my romantic partners.	1234567
25.	When my romantic partner wants to get too close, it makes me uncomfortable.	1234567
26.	I sometimes have difficulty building emotional closeness with my partner.	1234567
27.	I sometimes have difficulty building physical closeness with my partner.	1234567
28.	When I have concerns and problems, I find it challenging go to my partner for help and advice.	1234567
29.	Turning to my partner in times of need is something I find difficult to do	1234567

30.	I share very little about myself with my partner.	1234567
31.	I talking things over with my partner makes me uncomfortable or nervous	1234567
32.	I get nervous when my partners get too close.	1234567
33.	Depending on my romantic partners makes me uncomfortable.	1234567
34.	I do not find it easy to depend on my romantic partners.	1234567
35.	I do not find it easy to be affectionate with my romantic partner.	1234567
36.	I do not feel as though my partner really understands me or my emotional needs.	1234567

(Adapted from http://www.psych.uiuc.edu/~rcfraley/measures/ec-rritems.htm):

How to analyze your results:

The first eighteen questions reflect your responses to attachment-related anxiety. To determine whether or not you display any anxious preoccupied attachment tendencies, take your average of questions 1 to 18. The higher your score, the more attachment anxiety you exhibit.

Question 19-36 can be used to determine your attachment-avoidance related issues. To determine whether or not you display avoidant attachment tendencies, take the average of questions 19-36. The higher your score, the more avoidant attachment issues you have.

If you scored low on both the attachment- anxiety and attachment-avoidance questions, you likely exhibit a secure attachment style.

Multiple Attachment Styles

But what if you find yourself identifying with more than one attachment style? If this is the case, you are certainly not alone. As human beings, we are complex creatures, and our behaviour and tendencies can rarely be neatly categorized.

Even those among us who have a primarily secure attachment style may exhibit occasional avoidant or anxious tendencies. While it is possible to have more than one attachment style, and to fluctuate between them, it can be helpful to take a close look at your behaviour and tendencies to determine which style is the most dominant.

CHAPTER FOUR: HOW ATTACHMENT SHAPES OUR LOVE PERSONALITIES

As psychologist John Bowlby famously said, "What cannot be communicated to the mother cannot be communicated to the self."

This famous quote highlights the fact that those of us with attachment issues often have trouble understanding ourselves. We struggle to make sense of what it is we are feeling, and as a result, find it difficult to express our feelings to our partners and other loved ones.

Hopefully by now you are beginning to recognize the attachment style, or styles, that you exhibit. Perhaps you are beginning to make correlations between any attachment anxiety you have and the way you behave, both in relationships and in everyday life.

Let's take a look now at how our attachment styles can manifest into what we term *love personalities.* Through extensive research, marriage and family therapist Kay Yerkovich and her husband Milan Yerkovich have devised five love personalities that can help make sense of how we love. See if you can recognise yourself in any of these five love styles:

The Pleaser

Those of us who grow up to become pleasers were often raised with overly critical parents. As children, pleasers' primary goal was to keep their often-irritable parents happy and went out of their way to be good and do the right thing. All their actions were driven by a need to avoid provoking a negative response from their primary caregiver. These children rarely received comfort from their parent, and instead, devoted their time and energy to providing comfort to those they relied on for love and support.

As both adults and children, pleasers do their best to avoid conflict at all costs, even if that means refusing to stand their ground in an argument, or accepting responsibility for something they did not do. Pleasers are also prone to lying, in order to avoid confrontation or conflict.

The pleaser often finds it very difficult to say no, often leading them to do things they do not want to do.

As they grow, pleasers become adept at reading the moods of others. They see this as an integral part of avoiding conflict and keeping everyone happy.

In romantic relationships, this constant need to please can often lead to a breakdown. If a pleaser believes they are letting their partner down in any respect, they will often flee from relationships, unable to face conflict.

In trying to keep everyone happy, pleasers often spread themselves too thin, neglecting their own wellness and requirements. Pleasers put the needs of others before their own and often suffer from the belief that they are simply not good enough.

While caring about the needs of others is an honorable trait, pleasers need to remember to make time for themselves. In order to build strong relationships, they must learn to be honest about their feelings, even if that opens them up to conflict and disagreements. They must realize that always doing what is expected of them can lead to exhaustion and burnout.

The Pleaser generally identifies with an ***anxious ambivalent*** attachment style.

The Victim

Victims often grow up in a home full of chaos and insecurity. Their parents may be abusive or violent. As a coping mechanism, victims often attempt to disappear into the background, doing everything they can to avoid bringing attention to themselves. Hiding and staying silent become ways of slipping under the radar, in order to avoid provoking their angry or violent parents.

For victim children, reality can be unbearable. To cope, they often create a fantasy world in their heads, in which they can disappear into, allowing them respite from the horrors and struggles of the real world around them.

Victim children often grow up suffering from low self-esteem and depression. Often they will end up marrying someone who exhibits the same abusive behavior as their parents.

Because victims spend so much of their life surrounded by chaos, they come to see this as the norm. When they find themselves in situations without conflict, this can often be a source of stress. So used to existing in a state of chaos, the victim will often spend their time anticipating the next blow-up, with their mind constantly leaping to the worst-case scenario.

But it is possible for victims to cultivate secure and loving relationships. In order to do this, they must work on developing their sense of self-love and learn to stand up for themselves in difficult situations.

Victims generally identify with an *avoidant* attachment type.

The Controller

Children who become controllers usually come from homes in which there was little security or protection. They learn from a young age that, in order to survive, they must toughen up and take care of themselves.

As adults, controllers fear the vulnerability they felt during childhood resurfacing. In order to prevent this, they feel the need to be in control in every situation.

This need for naturally spills over into controllers' romantic relationships. They attempt to exercise control over their partner in order to avoid feeling vulnerable, humiliated or helpless. Controllers see their anger as a weapon, which can be wielded over their partner in order to remain in control. Stepping out of their comfort zone is a big challenge for controllers, as it causes them to feel weak and unsafe, often recalling negative experiences from their unprotected childhood.

Controllers often have a rigid personality, believing that there is only one way to do things, and that their way is right. Relationship-building can be a big challenge for controllers, as they often prefer to do things on their own. Diverting from "their way" of doing something can lead controllers to become angry and malicious.

For controllers to develop long-lasting, meaningful relationships, they need to learn how to develop trust in others and let go a little. As anger is often a big problem, they must learn to successfully manage this emotion, instead of using it to intimidate their partner.

Many controllers identify with a ***dismissive avoidant*** love attachment style.

The Vacillator

Vacillators often grow up in households with unpredictable parents, such as those who work long hours, or are rarely at home. They come to learn that their own needs are not the top priority for their often-busy parents. Craving attention, vacillators spend their energy seeking attention from their unpredictable caregivers. But when vacillators finally receive their parents' attention, they are often too angry or exhausted to properly receive it.

As adults, vacillators seek the reliable and consistent love they did not receive as children. One of their tendencies is to idealize new partners and relationships. While this can make for a blissful "honeymoon period," when the inevitable conflict arises (as it does in all relationships), they quickly grow disheartened, feel let down and allow doubts and insecurity to creep in.

Vacillators are often extremely sensitive, particularly when it comes to operating within a romantic relationship. They exhibit keen skills of perception, which allows them to easily observe changes in others – namely, their romantic partner.

For vacillators to succeed in building a secure and healthy relationship, it is essential that they learn to pace themselves. People with this love style are prone to throwing themselves into relationships too quickly, in their search for consistent love, opening themselves up to disappointment and hurt.

Many vacillators identify with an ***anxious ambivalent*** attachment style.

The Avoider

Those of us with an "avoider" love style often grew up with less affectionate and "hands-on" parents. They likely come from a household in which independence and self-reliance are cultivated and prized. Getting little comfort from their parents, or other caregivers, avoiders learn quickly to push their emotions and anxieties to the background, allowing them to focus on their day-to-day needs for survival. They learn from a young age how to take care of themselves.

This practice of disregarding their feelings leads avoiders to rely on logic, rather than emotion. While this can be a positive trait in some situations, it can also lead to them behaving detached and aloof. Being around people showing extreme emotions can make avoiders very uncomfortable.

To build healthy relationships, avoiders must learn to stop bottling up their feelings. By expressing their emotions and being honest with their partner, they will slowly develop trust.

As the name suggests, avoiders generally identify with ***dismissive avoidant*** or ***fearful avoidant*** love styles.

*

Each love style has its own set of unique challenges. Understanding your own attachment style and love personality will help you to identify and manage any negative behavioural patterns that surface within your romantic relationships. This is a powerful, and often life-changing exercise that can truly transform your relationships with those around you.

CHAPTER FIVE: DATING AND ATTACHMENT

D o you find yourself on an endless cycle of awkward first dates and relationships that fizzle out before they've even begun? Can you see the same patterns of behavior emerging in all your relationships – both your own behavior and that of your partner? Do you find yourself always dating the same kind of men or women? Or do you constantly find yourself sabotaging relationships the moment they show any kind of promise?

If your answer to any of these questions is yes, you've likely come to realize that your attachment style is to blame. Depending on our own tendencies, we are drawn to people who exhibit particular characteristics, which explains why we can constantly end up dating people with the same damaging traits and behaviors.

So what are we to do? Sit at home in front of the TV every night? Resign ourselves to a life of being alone? Not at all. Even for those of us with an insecure attachment style, dating doesn't need to be a struggle. It all comes down to understanding ourselves and, wherever possible, our partners.

By now, you're familiar with the traits of each attachment style and the love styles they give rise to. So when you're next with your partner, or on a date, use this information to determine the attachment style and corresponding traits, of your partner.

In this chapter, we will take a look at what you can expect when dating people with each love attachment style. We will then look at all the possible attachment style combinations and some of the challenges that each coupling may face – along with methods for managing conflict and working towards building a healthy, long-lasting relationship.

Dating Someone With a Secure Attachment Style

It goes without saying that dating someone with a secure attachment style can be far less stressful than someone who exhibits anxious or avoidant tendencies. A person with secure attachment will not be afraid to be upfront and honest about what they want. They will likely "put their cards on the table" in terms of what they want out of a relationship and where they see their life heading. A person who is secure will likely have no problem expressing interest if they wish to continue dating, and will not hesitate to be honest and tell you if they don't wish to continue seeing you.

Once the relationship is established, a secure lover will seek to integrate you into their life, through introducing you to their friends and family wherever possible. A secure lover will never try to keep you from knowing who they truly are, and will welcome your own efforts to share. When they speak about their experiences and memories, secure partners will also share how they felt at the time, fostering a deeper sense of understanding and stronger emotional intelligence.

A partner with a secure attachment style will likely be empathetic and honest, unafraid to share his or her true feelings, due to their strong sense of self-worth. Unlike the other attachment styles, secure partners do not have fears related to love, and they can often assist their avoidant or anxious partners in opening up, or feeling more secure within a relationship.

When conflict inevitably arises, a partner with a secure attachment style will not shy away from it, but will make an effort to understand your point of view, and work towards a compromise that will suit both of you. Secures partners have no difficulty showing anger, but they will seek to communicate their distress in a rational way. They will not suppress their unhappiness, nor will they hold grudges.

Secure partners differ from the other attachment styles in their ability to more accurately read the feelings of their partner. Their peaceful attachment style allows them to tune into others, making them not only better romantic partners, but also great parents, friends and colleagues. They will freely express both positive and negative feelings within a relationship, thanks to their heightened emotional intelligence.

It's estimated that a little under half the population exhibits a secure attachment style. However, thanks to their ability to form healthy, long-lasting relationships, you'll find less and less "secures" in the dating pool.

To recap, let's take a quick look at the characteristics you can expect when dating someone with a secure attachment style:

- A great ability to resolve conflict
- They are not threatened by criticism
- They are open and honest
- They have great communication skills
- They will not play games
- They are comfortable with physical and emotional closeness
- They are quick to forgive
- They see sex and emotional closeness as being intrinsically connected
- They treat their partners with love and respect
- They take responsibility for their partner's well-being

Dating Someone With an Anxious Preoccupied Love Attachment Style

Behind the secure attachment, anxious preoccupied is the next largest love style, meaning there is a good chance you will come across someone with these tendencies in the dating pool. It is estimated that up to 20% of the population belong to this attachment group.

As we have learned, an anxious preoccupied attachment style is formed when a child's early needs for attachment and security are not met, usually through an absent or overworked parent. The challenges they faced as children – intense efforts to gain their parents' attention, along with the accompanying anger, disappointment and frustration – often remain unresolved and unprocessed.

In a relationship, people with an anxious preoccupied love attachment style can be clingy, or needy, in an often unconscious attempt to make up for the attention they were denied at a young age.

Anxious preoccupied lovers can often be unreliable; a trait that manifests not only in romantic relationships, but also at school, work and among friends. Their internal conflict leads them to be self-centred, unable to notice the emotional messages they are being sent by those around them.

What anxious preoccupied people crave – and what they have been searching for all their life – is stable, patient and reliable love. They require constant reassurance of their partner's love, making them less likely to venture out into the world on their own, afraid that, when they return, this love will no longer be waiting. This need for constant attachment makes the anxious preoccupied type less likely to pursue their own individual goals, or go off on their own adventures.

When single, someone with an anxious preoccupied attachment style will desperately want a partner, throwing themselves into the dating pool again and again, in an often-frantic search for love.

If you find yourself dating someone with an anxious preoccupied attachment style, you will see them "put their best foot forward," doing their best to win your approval early, often to the point of trying too hard. They feel a need to constantly prove themselves, believing that they need to do this in order to maintain your interest.

As the relationship progresses, they will seek constant interaction and constant physical and emotional contact, which can be a challenge for their partner. Provided you are giving them the attention they crave, they will allow you to behave badly, even to the point of being cruel and manipulative. After all, in the eyes of the anxious preoccupied, negative attention is still attention, and that is what matters.

Anxious preoccupied partners have strong feelings, many of which are centred around their need for attention. They will often blame their partner for not providing them with the love and support they feel they need. Compounding this issue is the anxious preoccupied's inability to properly open up and honestly express their feelings. While it's true that people with this attachment style can be very emotionally expressive, they are often unable to get to the root of the problem and honestly convey what is causing their distress. This comes from a place of bot not understanding themselves, and also from a place of not feeling safe in the relationship. They fear that, by sharing who they truly are, they will scare their partner away.

People with an anxious preoccupied love style are at risk of settling into a dysfunctional and damaging relationship with a similarly damaged partner, which mirrors the parenting they experienced throughout their childhood. This often leads to co-dependency, a state which prevents both parties from maturing emotionally and moving past their issues. An anxious preoccupied partner will hate being alone, even for short periods of time.

When in a relationship, anxious preoccupied lovers may find themselves constantly thinking about their partner, having difficulty concentrating on anything else. Unsurprisingly, this leads to overthinking issues, and perceiving problems that do not exist They are also prone to putting their partner on a pedestal, and focusing only on their good traits. As they revere their partner, they tend to forget about their own skills and unique talents. They are often unwilling to leave relationships that are clearly failing, believing that this could be the only chance they ever have to find love. Coupled with this, they often have the belief that they can change their partner, in order to make them more compatible.

In the same way that children throw tantrums in order to gain attention, you'll find anxious preoccupied partners engaging in their own negative or "protest" behaviour in an attempt to secure your attention. This may include:

- Constant calling, texting and/or emailing
- Loitering at your workplace in hope of running into you
- Hostile behavior such as rolling their eyes or walking away when you try to speak to them
- Making empty threats about leaving
- Pretending to be unapproachable, such as leaving messages unanswered or pretending to be busy
- Attempting to make you feel jealous

So what does all this mean if you find yourself dating someone who exhibits these traits and tendencies? Is the relationship doomed to fail from the beginning? Not at all. The key to cultivating a successful relationship with an anxious preoccupied is building their feelings of security and independence. While much of this work must naturally come from your partner (we will discuss this further in following chapters) there are plenty of things you can do to assist in this process.

Remember that an anxious preoccupied person's issues stem from the lack of safety or consistency they received as a child. In order to cultivate security within the relationship, do your best to be consistent. Answer messages in a timely manner and be sure to be reliable, and keep your promises. When you behave "hot and cold," it can trigger your partner's old, deep-seated insecurities. They may respond through anger, seeking to punish you through the silent treatment, or even by breaking up with you.

When conflict arises in your relationship, as it inevitably will, be sure to let your partner know that having a fight does mean you are leaving them. People with an anxious preoccupied attachment style are prone to jumping to the worst-case scenario and, as they so deeply fear abandonment and rejection, their instinctive reaction to conflict is the adopting the belief that the relationship is about to end. In order to avoid the pain of rejection, they may even seek to end the relationship first. Be sure to let them know that, even though you are fighting, it does not change how much you love and care for them.

People with an anxious preoccupied attachment style have difficulty feeling assured in a relationship. So be sure to tell them how you feel on a regular basis. Be as honest and open about your feelings as possible. It could be as simple as a text to let them know you are thinking of them. Don't assume they know you love them. Anxious preoccupieds will rarely make this assumption on their own. Be proactive in telling them how you feel.

Above all, don't invalidate their feelings. Remember that their behaviours are often unconscious, and come from a place of trauma way back in their early years. Acknowledge that there is nothing foolish about the way they are feeling and, even though you may be able to see the situation logically, understand that this may be impossible for them. Do your best not to judge, instead offering a place in which they can feel safe and secure.

Dating Someone With a Dismissive Avoidant Love Attachment Style

Thanks to unreliable caregivers in childhood, people with a dismissive avoidant love style have a fear of intimacy, and a belief that they do not need attachments. However, as these beliefs and fears are subconscious, you will likely still come across several dismissive avoidants in the dating pool.

The lack of love and security dismissive avoidants receive as children often leads to an inflated sense of self-importance. They have grown up with no one to rely on but themselves, which leads them to believe that they don't need anyone else in order to survive and succeed.

People with dismissive avoidant love styles pride themselves on their independence and self-sufficiency. They believe that needing others is a weakness and a trait that will hold them back. They can be distant, hostile and condescending.

Dismissive advoidants have a tendency to end relationships without giving them a "real go." Often, they will hold an ideal in their mind of a previous relationship; an ideal to which they believe no one can ever measure up to. And when your relationship does end, the dismissive avoidant will act aloof, thanks to their belief that they are fine on their own.

In order to cultivate their protective shield of independence, dismissive avoidants often hate being asked to look inwards and examine their behaviour, both past and present. They will often struggle to remember their childhood, having repressed the negative memories that led to the formation of their dismissive behaviour. When they do recall attachment issues from their past, they often do so in a flippant or dismissive way, believing attachment is unimportant. They carry the belief that any negative experience – such as physical or emotional abuse from their parents – simply helped them become the strong, resilient person they are today.

The more you ask for attention and closeness, the more dismissive your partner will likely become. But of course, as humans, even dismissive avoidants have a biological need for connection. And when they are starved of this, they will engage in unhealthy behaviour in order to compensate. For example, single dismissive avoidants may become workaholics, or obsessed with hobbies or sports. In relationships, being separated from their partner for an extended period of time may elicit similar behaviour, only to have them act distant and hostile on their partner's return.

Dismissive avoidants will often seek to fulfil their biological needs for emotional and physical connection from less demanding partners

– often anxious preoccupied lovers who require constant attention, regardless of whether it is based on real intimacy and connection.

If you find yourself dating someone with a dismissive avoidant attachment style, you will likely find them charming at first. They know well what is expected of them when dating and can play the role perfectly at first. But dismissive avoidants' view subconsciously sees being attached to others as a negative thing. They compare all new relationships to that one unobtainable ideal and are prone to quickly discarding new relationships when they come time consuming or inconvenient.

If the relationship does continue, dismissive avoidants will find faults in you and, contrary to the behaviour of the anxious preoccupied, will focus only on your negative traits and shortcomings. But dismissive avoidants will go to great lengths to avoid talking about their feelings. The first inkling you have that something is wrong may well be when your dismissive partner breaks up with you.

But if you experience this, it is important to realize that you are not to blame. A dismissive avoidant's upbringing renders them incapable of tolerating real intimacy, and when anyone tries to get close to them, their knee-jerk response is to run away. While outwardly, the dismissive avoidant may seek to blame others for his or her relationship failures, the reality is that, at their core, his or her self-esteem is so low they do not believe themselves worthy of love and affection. If you succeed in breaking through a dismissive avoidant's defensive shield, catching a glimpse of their insecurities beneath, they will panic and run, seeking either solitude, or someone who does not realize they are not exactly what they seem.

In relationships, dismissive avoidant people engage in protective behaviour known as "distancing," in order to keep their partners from getting too close. These behaviours include:

- Not returning phone calls or messages
- Telling their partner they are not ready to commit, but staying together anyway

- Focusing on their partner's flaws
- Comparing their partner to their ex
- Flirting with others to introduce insecurity into the relationship
- Refusing to say "I love you"
- Pulling away after positive interactions. (For example, not calling after a great date.)
- Forming relationships that do not have a future, such as with someone who is married.
- Avoiding sex
- Not wanting to share a bed with their partner

So what should you do if you find yourself dating someone with a dismissive avoidant attachment style? While this attachment style can lead to potentially destructive and hurtful relationships, the first step in building a healthy relationship is understanding that this avoidant behaviour is not your fault. Understand that it comes from your partner's deep-seated beliefs that began to take root in the very first years of their life.

Firstly, understand that anger or throwing a tantrum might be the only way a dismissive avoidant is able to communicate his or her feelings. It may be tempting for you to respond with anger of your own. But this will only add fuel to the fire. Instead of engaging with this negative behaviour, take a step back. Walk away if you need to, and return to the issue when you feel you can operate with a clear head and a calm state of mind. Express your needs in an adult way, without making demands or issuing ultimatums. After all, this is a sure-fire to get a dismissive avoidant to run in the opposite direction!

Do your best to calmly come up with solutions to the conflict that will benefit you both. For example, perhaps you're angry that your avoidant partner has failed to return your messages for three days straight. Instead of attacking him or her, understand that this is simply a characteristic of their attachment style and is not intended to hurt you.

Ask that the next time he or she feels the need for space, they agree to let you know and to contact you the following day. This way, your partner will have the space they need, and you will not feel as though the relationship is being threatened.

People with dismissive avoidant attachment styles have a tendency to overthink things and get lost in their heads. To overcome this, it can be helpful to have dates that involve physical activity, such as hiking, playing sport or going dancing. The physical exertion will cause your partner to get out of their head and be present in the moment and they will be more likely to connect and form a lasting bond.

Having an avoidant partner requires patience. While you may logically see that opening up and sharing their feelings will be beneficial, understand that this process does not come easily to people with an avoidant attachment style. Allow them personal space when they need it and be sure to be engaged and present when they are finally ready to share. The other key thing to remember is that for many avoidants, learning to share their feelings can be as simple as just naming their emotion. By encouraging this simple step, it can open the door to greater connection and openness.

Though they may not always act like it, the reality is that dismissive avoidants want – and need – love just as much as the rest of us. For dismissive avoidants to cultivate a healthy relationship, it is essential that they learn to open up and share with their partner. The exercises in the following chapter will be of particular benefit to couples with a dismissive avoidant partner.

Dating Someone with a Fearful Avoidant Attachment Style

Just like dismissive avoidants, fearful avoidant attachment styles come from a deep distrust of a person's caregiver. Because of the similarities between these two attachment styles, dating a fearful avoidant can be a similar experience to dating someone with a dismissive avoidant attachment style. Unlike dismissive avoidants however, people with a fearful avoidant attachment style do not have the defensive shield of high self-esteem. They accept that they both want and need intimacy and attachment in their life.

Problems can arise, however, as the relationship develops. Fearful avoidants crave intimacy, leading them get closer to their partner. But when they do, their old fears kick in and they suddenly feel the need to pull away. This can lead to an endless series of short relationships, in which the fearful avoidant seeks closeness, only to flee when they actually receive it.

In the dating pool, fearful avoidants often put on a façade; a front they believe makes them more likeable. They can maintain this "false self" even in moments of intimacy. Just like dismissive avoidants, fearful avoidants have difficulty sharing their feelings with their partners. They are also characterized by weakened empathy, meaning they are often difficult to communicate with.

Dating someone with a fearful avoidant attachment style has many similarities with a dismissive avoidant partner. It can be helpful to go back and read the previous section.

If you find yourself dating someone with a fearful avoidant personality, once again, understand that their behaviour is not a reflection of you. Their trait stems from the damaging belief that they are not worthy of love and affection.

Just as with dismissive avoidants, people with this attachment type will greatly benefit from learning to open up and reveal their true selves to their partners. The exercises in the following chapter will be of particular benefit to people with a fearful avoidant attachment style.

Attachment Type Combinations

Knowing both the attachment styles of yourself and your partner can be of incomparable benefit to your relationship. Being able to anticipate the behaviour of both parties within a relationship – and the possible obstacles you will face can help smooth the path to a healthier, long-lasting connections.

Let's take a look at what to expect when people with each attachment type form a couple:

Secure + Secure

While secure couples in relationships have problems just like everybody else, their relationship is often characterized by great communication and empathy. They resolve conflicts more easily and know that they can rely on each other, in good times and bad.

The secure + secure coupling is the most common type of relationship, owing both to the large number of people in the population with secure attachment styles, and secures' abilities to cultivate healthy, long-lasting relationships.

Anxious Preoccupied + Secure

In this relationship combination, the anxious preoccupied partner is likely to test the patience of the secure partner, by seeking regular assurance. If the secure partner does not act quickly, the anxious preoccupied partner can become anxious and stressed. Despite their inherent securities, this behaviour can test the patience of the secure partner and can cause them to act distantly or pull away, much as a dismissive avoidant would.

However, a secure partner can be of great benefit to an anxious preoccupied person. The secure can cultivate their partner's trust in the relationship through patient and constant reassurance.

In such a combination, the secure partner can often feel as though they themselves are responsible for the upkeep and security of the relationship. The anxious preoccupied's insecurities can cause them to become self-centred, causing the secure partner to feel as though their loved one is not invested in the relationship.

Through gentle reassurance from the secure partner, however, this problem should improve over time.

Dismissive Avoidant + Secure

When partnered with a dismissive avoidant, a person will often experience distance and coldness within a relationship. This behaviour can cause even the most secure of people to feel attachment anxiety, leading them to question their self-worth. Even though the secure's requests for assurance will likely be reasonable, the dismissive avoidant partner will usually not respond to these requests.

In order for such a combination to work, the secure partner must be aware of their partner's issues, and demonstrate enormous amounts of patience in order to cultivate more security and openness with the relationship.

It is equally important for the dismissive avoidant partner to recognize the role they are playing in the relationship's struggles and do their best to respond positively to their partner's requests, even if it at first feels like a challenge.

If this does not happen, it will likely be the secure partner who ends the relationship. They are comfortable and confident enough in their own abilities and self-worth to know there is someone out there who will treat them right.

Fearful Avoidant + Secure

This combination has much in common with the dismissive avoidant + secure pairing. The difference is, however that it is likely to be the fearful avoidant partner who ends the relationship at the first sign of trouble. This behaviour comes about thanks to the fearful avoidant's fear of being seen for who they really are. They are afraid of loss and believe that ending the relationship on their own terms will be far less painful than the rejection from their partner. They often come to believe that this rejection is inevitable, once the secure breaks through the fearful avoidant's façade.

Dismissive Avoidant + Anxious Preoccupied

This potentially damaging combination is one of the most common. Because of an unconscious need to replay the events of their childhood, the anxious preoccupied will seek out the inconsistent attention provided by the dismissive avoidant. The dismissive avoidant undervalues their partner, while the anxious preoccupied overvalues them, leading to a relationship characterised by stress and anxiety.

While the dismissive avoidant likes to shy away from intimacy and connection, their needy partner will act to confirm the dismissive avoidant's view that all people are clingy. This confirmation makes the dismissive avoidant more comfortable in the relationship than they would otherwise be, and they often settle in to this coupling for the long-haul.

Meanwhile, the anxious preoccupied partner is unhappy with the sporadic attention doled out by their partner, but they are too afraid of being alone to do anything about it.

These negative patterns can be extremely difficult to break, largely because each partner sees the other as the cause of the relationship's problems.

But change is possible. If you find yourself in this coupling, return to the previous chapter and take a look at the ways of managing partners with avoidant and anxious attachment styles. The avoidant partner must learn to be more consistent and assuring in the relationship, while the anxious partner must work on building their inner-assurance and self-worth, instead of constantly relying on their partner for validation.

As in all couplings, open and honest communication, along with empathy is the key to making this relationship work.

Fearful Avoidant + Anxious Preoccupied

This coupling is among the most negative and damaging. It is also one the most insecure couplings. The anxious preoccupied partner's constant need for attention will scare off the fearful avoidant partner, who will usually be unwilling to be involved in a relationship in which they are constantly fending off intimacy.

If the fearful avoidant partner acquiesces to their partner's need for closeness, it will likely trigger their anxiety. Conversely, if they remain in their comfort zone and keep their distance, the anxious preoccupied partner will respond by increasing their requests for attention.

Anxious Preoccupied + Anxious Preoccupied

This is another coupling that very rarely has a happy ending. The often self-absorbed anxious preoccupieds will have trouble anticipating the needs and desires of their partner. With both partners having a deep-seated need for attention and closeness, it is unlikely – although not impossible – that they will be able to satisfy each other's desires.

Fearful Avoidant + Dismissive Avoidant

This partnership is an uncommon one, due to both parties being bad at positive attachment. Even though, on the surface, it may appear that both partners want a less "hands-on" approach to the relationship, the fearful avoidant has a deep-seated need for attachment that the dismissive avoidant will rarely fill.

Dismissive Avoidant + Dismissive Avoidant

Unsurprisingly, this coupling is very rare. As cultivating a relationship requires communication – something dismissive avoidants seek to avoid – a relationship between two people with this attachment style rarely gets off the ground. If they do manage to form a relationship, they are prone to ending it at the first hint of conflict, in order to avoid having to communicate and resolve the issue.

Fearful Avoidant + Fearful Avoidant

This is the most uncommon matching, but this is primarily due to the fact that there is only a small number of fearful avoidant people in the general population. The fearful avoidant's difficulties with regards to communication and self-esteem will make this coupling a challenge, however it is not necessarily doomed to fail. As both parties have a deep-seated need for intimacy, there is the chance that they can satisfy this need for each other. They have a better chance of being successful if they understand the challenges faced by both themselves and their partner – something which is true for every coupling.

*

It is interesting – and often encouraging – to note that we are not necessarily stuck with one love style forever. Over time, our tendencies and inclinations within romantic relationships can evolve as we grow as lovers and people. So if your relationship has hit a rough patch, don't be discouraged. Just because you and your partner may have seemingly in-compatible attachment styles, it does not necessarily mean you have to end things. Instead, look at it as an opportunity for you both to develop as people and strengthen the bonds of your relationship.

CHAPTER SIX: WORKING WITH YOUR ATTACHMENT STYLE TO FIND YOUR LIFE PARTNER

N ow that you've recognized your attachment style, and that of your partner, you can use this information to strengthen your romantic relationships. Identifying and understanding the struggles we face in relationships, and the traps we are likely to fall into helps us see and manage problems before they manifest and ultimately doom the relationship.

The reality is that over half of us do not exhibit a secure attachment style, instead exhibiting one of the two "damaged" styles – anxious or avoidant. On top of this, those of us with an avoidant or anxious love style have an above-average chance of falling in love with someone from the other damaged side. Unless we are careful, being with someone from the "opposite" side of the love style spectrum can aggravate our insecurities and cause us to act rashly or put up defenses.

Here are a few things to keep in mind about your own behavior when it comes to dating and building relationships:

If You Have an Avoidant Attachment Style...

- Particularly if you are in a relationship with someone who exhibits anxious preoccupied tendencies, learn to recognize the extent to which you check out emotionally, particularly in tense situations, or when your partner is offering or seeking closeness.
- Begin to recognize the way you prefer sex and physical intimacy with strangers, rather than with your significant other. You may also begin to notice how uncomfortable you feel when cuddling,

kissing or during any other displays of affection. It is also highly likely that you don't like the light on during sex and intimacy.

- Notice your behavioral patterns that lead you to sabotage the chance for building healthy, long-term relationships. Can you see that you are afraid of what you really want? How does this internal conflict make you feel? Do your best to have compassion and forgiveness for yourself.

- Think back to your childhood. Can you see where this behavior may have taken root? In all likelihood, closeness would have been a frightening thing, because those you relied on for love and support continually let you down. Can you see the way you adopted a strategy in order to protect yourself from harm?

- Remember, the present is different from the past. By bringing in behaviors driven by fear, you are ruining your chance at a happy present and future. Can you see the way that these behaviors belong to the past? Can you that they do not belong in your present and future?

- With this in mind, now take a closer look at your partner's behavior. Perhaps it may seem as though they are behaving aggressively, and are causing you to feel upset, and perhaps even afraid. Take a moment to reframe their behavior. Understand that they are doing what they are doing because they want to be with you, and, if they have an anxious preoccupied attachment style, they likely have difficulty expressing this in a healthier way. Next time they attack or nag you, try and look beneath the irritation of this and see this as their deep-seated need for love.

If You Have an Anxious Attachment Style...

- If you are an anxious preoccupied person with a partner who exhibits avoidant tendencies, firstly bear in mind that things are usually not as bad as they seem. Perhaps your partner is being quiet and withdrawn. Likely, your mind is jumping to conclusions, interpreting this as a lack of love, or deep-seated troubles within the relationship. But take a moment to consider that this is likely not the case. Your partner's quietness is more than likely just that – a momentary need for peace and stillness. There is every chance it has nothing to do with you at all. Recognize that those with avoidant love styles require greater amounts of personal space. If your partner exhibits these tendencies, it is far more to do with them, than you.

- However, it is not unreasonable for you to want more closeness and intimacy from a partner who can often seem aloof and detached. There is nothing inherently needy about this. But it is important to take note of *how* you are asking your partner for this intimacy. Are you being too direct? In all likelihood, you are probably doing so with too much rage and desperation. Recognize the frightening affect this can have on an avoidant partner, and tread lightly when requesting closeness. Accepting, and even creating, a little more distance between you and your partner can have a positive effect on your relationship.

- Above all, recognize that your partner's behavior does not come from a place of spite. He or she is simply acting out negative behavioral patterns learned in childhood – just as you are.

Increasing Your Attachment Security

While many of us are not lucky enough to naturally have a secure relationship attachment style, there are many things we can do to build our attachment security. Let's take a look at few of the ways we can work with our partners to build up our own – and each other's – security within our relationships:

Asking Questions:

Asking each other questions can be an invaluable way of opening up to your partner and sharing details about yourself that even you might not have previously been aware of. A structured questionnaire can take away the overwhelming aspect of having to come up with your own questions. Here is a selection of questions, beginning rather light-hearted and increasing in emotional intensity. Particularly if you or your partner find it difficult to open up, you might choose to begin with a few of the early questions, moving down the list as far as you feel comfortable. These are a great way to get to know your partner a little better – and to know your yourself a little better in the process!

1. Who are your top five dream dinner guests?
2. Would you like to be famous? Why? And in what way?
3. Do you ever rehearse conversations of telephone calls? If so, why?
4. Describe your perfect day.
5. When was the last time you sang a song? Was it to yourself, or to someone else?
6. If you could live to the age of 90 and retain either the mind or body of a 30 year old, which would you choose and why?
7. Do you have an inkling about the way you are going to die?
8. What are three things you think we have in common?
9. What are you the most grateful for in your life?

10. If you could change one thing about your childhood, what would it be?

11. Tell me your life story in three minutes, in as much detail as possible.

12. If you could suddenly acquire one new ability, what would it be and why?

13. If a crystal ball could accurately tell you the future, would you want to know it? Why or why not?

14. What have you always dreamed of doing? Why haven't you done it yet?

15. What is your greatest achievement?

16. What do you value most in a friend? A partner?

17. Describe your most treasured memory.

18. Describe your most horrible memory.

19. If you knew you were going to die in one year's time, what would you change about the way you are living your life?

20. How important are love and affection in your life?

21. List five positive traits about your partner.

22. How close do you feel to your family? How do you think your childhood compares to other people's?

23. How positive or negative is your relationship with your mother?

24. Make up three statements about things you and your partner are sharing right now. For example: "We are both sitting on this sofa…"

25. What is the one thing you wish you could share with another person?

26. What is the one thing you need your partner to know about you in order to become closer to them?

27. Tell your partner three things you really like about them. Be honest.

28. What is your most embarrassing moment?

29. When was the last time you cried? Was it by yourself or in front of another person?

30. What do you believe is too serious to ever be joked about?

31. If you were to die today with no chance of communicating to anyone ever again, what is the one thing you wished you'd shared with someone?

32. Besides you loved ones, what are three things you would rescue if your house was one fire? Why?

33. Which of your loved ones' deaths would you find the most difficult to handle? Why?

34. Tell your partner about a personal problem you are having and ask their advice.

    This exercise can also be done between two couples. Studies have shown that asking these questions when doubling dating can increase not only closeness between the couples, but within the couples at the same time.

Engaging in Joint Activites

As discussed in the previous chapter, engaging in physical activities with your partner can be a great way of getting out of your heads and being in present in the moment, which can allow for greater bonding. Take this a step further by taking part in activities designed for couples. You might like to consider:

- Couples yoga
- Get a couples massage
- Visit each other's hometowns
- Choose a new TV series together and binge watch it
- Create a scrapbook of your relationship
- Have a picnic
- Play mini golf
- Cook dinner together

- Take a trip somewhere neither of you have been
- Volunteer together
- Watch the sun rise
- Dress up in a couple's costume for Halloween
- Climb a mountain or go on a hike
- Start a new tradition together
- Go bowling
- Go horseback riding
- Create a music playlist as the soundtrack to your relationship
- Take a bubble bath
- Go to the beach
- Take a dance class
- Go camping
- Sit in front of an open fire
- Go on a tandem bike ride
- Do a fun run together
- Read each other your favourite book

Keep a Journal

Writing in a journal each night can be a great way to make sense of your emotions and feelings. Journaling has been scientifically proven to reduce stress and anxiety, and can provide you with greater mental clarity, greater problem-solving abilities and a greater ability to manage conflict.

But journaling and sharing the contents with your partner can also have a profound effect on your relationship's security. It provides a platform for greater honesty and openness, and improves trust between you and your partner. Reading from the written page can also take the stress and spontaneity out of sharing your feelings, which can be of particular benefit to those with avoidant personalities, who will likely find this exercise a challenge.

Reflecting on Positive Relationships

Research has proven that the act of simply focusing on your previous positive relationships can have a profound positive influence on your current romantic relationship. This could be done either through journaling, discussion with your partner, or even just taking a few moments for yourself to conjure up these positive memories.

*

The abovementioned activities and questionnaire is likely to have a greater effect of increasing the attachment security of those with an avoidant attachment style, as these exercises encourage openness and honesty, while pushing participants out of their comfort zones.

Hopefully, the above suggestions have shown that developing a more secure attachment style does not need to be strenuous. Increasing the security of your attachment with your loved one can be an enjoyable experience. And it can be as simple as learning to open up and share a few details about your lives. Remember to above all, do your best to be honest and show compassion, both to yourself and your partner.

CHAPTER SEVEN: HOW TO FEEL GOOD WITHOUT PARTNERSHIP

Given the images our media constantly bombards us with, it's easy to develop the belief that there is something wrong with being single. So much of what we see on TV, in magazines, and in films seems to suggest that the one goal in life is to find a loving partner and settle down and have a family. And then there's an ever-growing number of social media sites which portray endless collections of photos of our friends and acquaintances showing off their loving partners, or their beautiful kids… Little wonder many of us see romantic attachment as our main goal or achievement in life.

But the nature of life means that we are all bound to be single at one time or another. This could be due to luck on the dating scene, commitments in other areas of our lives, or even death and bereavement.

For some of us, being single can be a traumatic process. This may be due to our attachment style, and/or the circumstances that led to us being in the situation. It is important to develop skills to cope with being single, or else we may find ourselves heading blindly into unsuitable and damaging relationships, driven by the fear of being alone. It may lead us to settle, agreeing to spend our life with someone we do not love, or who does not love us in return.

While some of us relish time alone, and may choose to be single, many people prefer, and even crave the company of other people. While there is nothing inherently wrong with this – after all, it comes down to our personality and attachment styles – it is important not to fall to pieces the moment we find ourselves alone.

Attachment Style and Single Status

Our upbringing, unsurprisingly, can have a big effect on the way we respond to being alone. Our response to this situation is due largely to what is termed our *family script.* If you grew up in a large family with people constantly around you, you may have a more difficult time adjusting to being on your own. Conversely, those who grew up with distant or absent parents are able to more quickly adjust when they find their relationships ending.

But as we have learned, our attachment styles can always be changed and improved. It's just a matter of understanding ourselves more thoroughly, and determining why we have particular behaviours or fears.

So if you are experiencing stress over the thought of being single, or alone, here are a few strategies to help manage the anxiety:

Facing Your Fears

Start with asking yourself exactly what it is about being single that scares you. Is it the belief that people will judge you? If so, this can be a good opportunity to recognize how much you are letting other people's opinions of you inform your sense of self-worth.

Perhaps you are afraid that not having a partner will cause you to miss out on a lot of things. In this case, you could examine why you feel you need a partner to take part in experiences. Are there are things you have been waiting for a partner to do, such as traveling, when you can just as easily do them on your own?

It's also worth examining just where this fear has come from. Can you identify incidences from your past that may have contributed to your fear of being alone? Perhaps, like the above example, you grew up surrounded by your large family, and not having company feels strange and unnatural. Or maybe there was an incident in your early childhood that sparked this fear – for example, you may have wandered off as a child and lost your mother in a shopping mall.

Understanding the underlying causes of this fear can go a long way towards addressing and removing them.

Understanding What You Want

As we have discussed in many aspects throughout this book, understanding yourself and your desires is of great benefit when it comes to managing your instinctive thoughts and behaviours.

If you find yourself struggling to be single, take the time to really ask yourself what you want from life. This can be with regards to your goals and aspirations, and also as related to your attachment style. What is it that your attachment style demands? Do you need validation from others in order to feel secure in yourself? Or do you crave alone time? (If you have not done so, go to Chapter Three in order to determine your love attachment style.)

Understanding yourself in this way can help you feel more secure in yourself, and less like you need another person to "complete" you.

This is also a great opportunity to explore new interests and hobbies. What have you always wanted to try, but have never done? Is there a hobby from your past that used to bring you joy? Can you incorporate this back into your life?

Relationship Counselling

While it might seem silly, the reality is that relationship counselling is not just for couples. As we know, one of the most important relationships we have is with ourselves. If you are struggling with your single status, it might be worth seeking the help of a qualified counsellor in order to get to the root of exactly what it is that is causing your distress. See Chapter Ten for some tips on how to find the right counsellor or therapist for you.

Being Happy and Single

Depending on your desires, personality and attachment style, the thought of being happy and single might seem impossible to achieve. But the reality is that there are plenty of men and women who are extremely happy without a partner, both through personal choice and external circumstances.

There are plenty of benefits to being single – you have the freedom to decide what you're going to do and when, you rarely have to compromise, plus you get the whole bed to yourself!

But despite this, it can be difficult to be happy and single when you really want a partner. Society teaches us that we must find love in order to be happy. But in reality, it is the other way around. When we are happy with ourselves and our lives, we are far more likely to attract love.

So let's look at a few of the techniques that can be employed if you find your single status is getting you down:

Engage in mindful and meaningful activities.

Let's break this one down, as it contains two elements. When we're single, it's a great opportunity to engage in activities that make us happy. After all, we don't have to seek anyone's approval, or compromise with a partner about how we will spend our weekend! As discussed in the previous section, it can be of great benefit to take some time to identify activities and experiences that you love, or have always wanted to do. Rather than sitting at home obsessing over your single status, or the next series of awkward first dates you'll have to go on, get out in the world and take part in activities and experiences that are meaningful for you.

So what does it mean to be mindful, when you're engaging in these activities? Basically, it means being present in the situation, not lost in your thoughts, or in some fantasy world. If you find yourself drifting into your head, a great exercise to cultivate mindfulness is to focus on all five of your senses. Mentally list three things you can see – and be specific. Rather than just saying "I see a bird," take time to describe the bird to yourself: "I see the white tips on the feathers of that bird…" etc. Now do the same for each of your five senses. What do you hear, smell, feel and even taste?

Recognise it's okay to do things alone- and then do them!

When it feels as though everyone else in the world is happily coupled up, it can be difficult to get out and do things without company. But doing things alone can be a liberating experience. Go to the movies. Go shopping. Go out for a meal. Each time you do this, it will become easier and easier.

Take time to foster your other relationships

Despite what you may have led yourself to believe, your significant other is not the only key relationship in your life. Especially while you are single, take the time to cultivate relationships with the other special people in your life. Spend time with family, friends and colleagues in order to strengthen your relationship with them. Give your undivided attention to others when you are with them- don't be distracted thinking about your ex or your single status.

You can also use this opportunity to meet new people and cultivate new interests. (We will discuss this in more details in Chapter Nine.) And, importantly, allow yourself to meet people without viewing everyone as a potential partner.

Recognise that not all of your thoughts are based in reality.

Particularly for those of us with an anxious preoccupied love attachment style, you may find being single causes an endless cycle of inner dialogue to go charging through your head. Likely, it's filled with negative and self-deprecating thoughts along the lines of: *"I'm not good enough," "I'll never find love,"* or *"I'm so unattractive."*

If you find yourself thinking such things, take a moment to step back and see these thoughts as what they are: your own misinterpretation of reality, not facts.

Next time you find yourself entertaining this negative dialogue, replace it with a more positive belief. For example: *"I'll never find love"* could be replaced with *"today I will meet someone incredible."* Repeat this new belief to yourself in the form of an affirmation, or mantra. Say it to yourself over and over, either aloud or in your head. You can even write your new positive beliefs down and put them in places where you will see them often, such as on your bathroom mirror, on your desk at work, or inside your car. In time, you will find your negative inner dialogue replaced with these far more positive and productive beliefs.

Accept your emotions and allow yourself to really feel them.

Understand what you are feeling – give a name to your emotions. Is it grief? Embarrassment? Hopelessness? Joy? Do you feel as though you need to cry? Allow yourself to do so without feeling guilty. You will likely feel much better afterwards, and letting those emotions out is far healthier than bottling them up inside.

Understand how being in a relationship would change you – and make those changes now.

Take some time to determine exactly how being in a relationship would change your behaviour. Would you allow yourself to relax and feel less stressed? Or maybe you would no longer feel the need to spend an hour doing your make-up each morning.

Once you have identified these actions, start doing them now. Cultivate a sense of relaxation through activities such as mediation or yoga. Allow yourself to be that person who spends five minutes on their makeup before they run out the door.

This also applies to achieving your life goals. Are you waiting for that perfect partner to travel the world with? Why wait? Traveling solo can provide you with the most amazing experiences for growth and self-understanding. And who knows, you may even meet someone amazing in the place you least expect!

The same goes with having children. If your fear of being alone stems from your need to have a family, consider the possibility of doing it solo. Fostering, adoption and egg freezing are all valid avenues for exploration.

Don't put unnecessary pressure on any dates you might have

Especially if you have been single for a long time, or exhibit anxious attachment tendencies, it can be tempting to blow things out of proportion when you finally land a date. We can convince ourselves that this will be the one, placing an unnecessary amount of pressure on ourselves to not ruin what we see as our one chance at happiness.

On top of this added pressure, fantasizing about our dates, and convincing ourselves they are The One can be dangerous. It means we are often shut off to any negative behaviours and we may convince ourselves we can be happy with them, even in the face of red flags. This can lead us into unsatisfying and even damaging or abusive relationships.

Instead of focusing the future when you're on a date, remember the value of mindfulness, and focus on the present. Ensure you are fully present during the date, without focusing on past experiences or present fantasies.

*

Next time you find yourself without a romantic partner, focus on all the positive aspects of being single. Use it as a time to really understand yourself and your desires and for really exploring what makes you tick. Above all, allow yourself to recognize that we do not need romantic attachment in order to feel complete and happy.

CHAPTER EIGHT: HOW OUR ATTACHMENT STYLE AFFECT OUR FRIENDSHIPS

By now, it should be evident just how deeply our attachment style can affect our romantic relationships, along with our relationships with our parents and/or children. But our attachment style can also have a significant impact on our friendships and wider social networks. This includes our interactions with friends in person, along with our behaviours on social media sites such as Facebook.

Attachment Style and Friendship

The table below gives us a quick overview of the way the both our self-esteem (our opinion of ourselves) and our sociability (our opinion of others) is reflected in our love attachment style. We can use this as the basis for understanding our challenges and instinctive responses when faced with social situations, such as making or interacting with friends:

		Self Esteem (Our opinion of ourselves)	
Sociability (Our opinion of others)		**Positive**	**Negative**
	Positive	Secure love attachment style	Anxious preoccupied love attachment style

	Negative	Dismissive avoidant love attachment style	Fearful avoidant love attachment style

Friendship for Secure Attachment Personalities

As we have discussed in earlier chapters, people with a secure attachment style have a heightened emotional intelligence which allows them to communicate effectively with those around them. They are able to interpret both verbal and non-verbal cues, giving them strong empathetic skills. For this reason, people with secure attachment styles generally have no problem instigating and maintaining friendships. They make reliable friends and colleagues and flourish in group environments.

Friendship for Anxious Preoccupied Personalities

The anxious preoccupied's desperate need for attention and validation within romantic relationships also shows itself among friends.

People with an anxious preoccupied attachment style often feel as though they are giving far more to their friends than they are receiving. As those of us with these tendencies can be very emotionally expressive, we like to show our friends just how much they mean to us – and can occasionally overdo it. Anxious preoccupieds often see themselves as less valuable than their friends, and will behave accordingly. But for secures who don't view their friend as a "lesser person" than themselves, this anxious preoccupied behaviour can be difficult to understand. As a result, anxious preoccupieds often have difficulty building close connections with their friends.

If you have this attachment style, you may find yourself drawn towards friends who also exhibit anxious preoccupied tendencies. This will result in a friendship in which you both go out of your way to ensure the other knows how much you mean to them. While this can work, it is often characterised by desperation and neediness, and does not lead to the healthiest of relationships.

People with this attachment style are unlikely to maintain friendship with avoidant types, as the anxious need for attention is likely to drive the other person away before the friendship has time to develop.

Friendship for Dismissive Avoidant Personalities

While the way dismissive avoidants relate to their friends is completely opposite to anxious preoccupied personalities, the result is the same: a lack of close friendships. As we have learned, dismissive avoidants prize themselves on their independence and their perceived belief that they do not need anyone else in order to prosper. This can cause them to be distant and dismissive – something their secure friends will perceive as coldness, disinterest or even rudeness.

Friendship for Fearful Avoidant Personalities

While we all have versions of ourselves that we put out into the public eye, fearful avoidant personalities are adept at presenting a carefully cultivated persona, or *false self* when showing themselves to the world. This façade is a defense mechanism to prevent any spontaneous display of emotion and to keep their innermost feelings hidden away.

People who consider themselves friends with a fearful avoidant personality can often find themselves surprised and hurt when distress causes the fearful avoidant's "mask" to fall away. Their friends will then discover that the true personality of the person they had believed themselves close to was little more than a lie.

As a result of this false self, the fearful avoidant often has a group of friends that has been attracted to his or her fake persona and has little idea who they really are. When their true self is revealed in times of crisis, they may find they have no one who truly understands them – or perhaps even likes them – and consequently, they have no one on whom they can really rely.

Not being able to be vulnerable with friends who are vulnerable with you puts a strain on the relationship, making close friendships a challenge for fearful avoidants. It is important for people with this attachment type to recognise that real intimacy and friendship are based on loyalty and honesty. Pretending to be something you are not – while it can be an effective defense mechanism – will leave you with few friends you can count on in times of trouble.

Tie Strength and Multiplexity

Researchers at Australia's Deakin University and the Middle East Technical University in Turkey have determined the role of attachment styles as related to our friendship groups and social networks.

Their study examines "tie strength" and "multiplexity" within their subjects' social networks.

"Tie strength" refers to how close the ties in your network are; in other words, how comfortable you feel going to your friends for love and support in times of emotional distress. It also takes into consideration how often subjects interact with those in their network.

"Multiplexity" refers to having many different roles fulfilled by the same members of a subject's network. For example, a person who is both a colleague and a fellow member of a sports team has a high level of multiplexity. Similarly, if a subject feels close enough to a work colleague to go to them for advice and support, it also shows a high level of multiplexity.

Within an Avoidant Style...

The study shows that people with avoidant attachment styles have a weaker tie strength to members of their social network. This makes sense, given the avoidant's tendencies to shy away from affection. Similarly, avoidant behaviour also leads to lower multiplexity within friendships, meaning the bond an avoidant has with their friends and colleagues is weaker and less reliable. They are less likely to actively maintain ties and are more likely to actively dissolve their friendships.

Within an Anxious Attachment Style...

Those with an anxious preoccupied attachment style are also likely to see the frequent dissolution of friendship ties. However, in their case, it is likely to be instigated by their contacts, rather than by themselves. As we know, people with an anxious attachment style have a need for constant attention and validation. This behaviour can be smothering, leading to their friends and contacts to step away and dissolve the friendship.

Size of Your Social Network

You may assume that the larger a person's friendship network – either on or offline – the more popular and secure they are. However, this is not always the case.

Think about the size of your own social network. If you have hundreds, or even thousands, of connections on sites such as Facebook, think about how often you connect with the majority of people in this network. In all likelihood, not very often. The sheer numbers involved usually make this far too difficult. Similarly, if you have a huge circle of friends in "real life," it can be difficult to maintain close and meaningful relationships with all of them.

Studies support this, proving that the larger the friendship network, the weaker the ties and multiplexity of those connections.

Does this mean we should cull our Facebook pages and cut down our number of friends? Not necessarily. But it is important to recognize social media connections can never take the place of real life friendships. While it can be easier to cultivate friendships behind the safety of the computer screen, putting yourself out into the real world and facing the challenges thrown up by your attachment style is the only way to build valuable, long-lasting friendships.

Increasing your Attachment Security Among Friends

So how can we go about increasing our attachment security with regards to making and maintaining lasting friendships?

Remember those questions we discussed in Chapter Six as a way of developing intimacy between you and your romantic partner? These are just as effective when it comes to really getting to know your friends, or anyone you are seeking to build a deeper connection with. You can also make up your own list of questions, in order to avoid answers becoming routine.

If asking these questions makes you shy or uncomfortable, do your best to focus on the answers given by your friend, rather than your own responses. After all, showing interest in others and making them the focus of attention is a great way to make a person feel valuable and showing them you care.

In the following chapter we will be looking at ways to both build new friendships and maintain existing friendships, regardless of your attachment style.

CHAPTER NINE: HOW TO MAKE GREAT FRIENDS REGARDLESS OF YOUR ATTACHMENT STYLE

Making friends gets more and more difficult as we get older. Sociologists put this down to a number of reasons. Firstly, building friendships takes time. Think of all the hours you spent with your friends at school. Being forced to spend day after day together was what led your relationship to develop from being class-mates to becoming friends. But as adults, our lives are often so busy with work, children and numerous other responsibilities that we simply don't have as much time to cultivate friendships as we did when we were young. In addition, we generally spend much less time in one place than we did back in our school days. As adults, the only place we spend large proportions of our time is often our workplace, and some of us are reluctant to build friendships with our colleagues.

Then there's the issue of energy. Spending time with new people can be a major energy drain, especially if you suffer from an insecure attachment style. In today's modern life, so many of us are at risk of burnout, so we are understandably reluctant to introduce more stress into our lives.

But while making – and keeping – friends as a busy adult can be a challenge, it is well worth the effort. Let's take a look at some of the many benefits of friendship:

The Benefits of Friendship

- Being around friends improves your mood. Surrounding your-self with positive, happy people makes you feel better, and is proven to increase positivity and optimism.

- Having friends helps you reach your goals. Encouragement from those around you can boost willpower, while sharing your goals and aspirations with others helps hold you accountable.

- Having friends reduces stress and depression. Studies have shown that an active social life can boost your immune system. It also reduces isolation, which is a major contributor to depression and stress.

- Having friends mean you have someone to rely on in difficult times, such as unemployment, bereavement, illness, or difficulties in your romantic relationship.

- Surrounding yourself with friends can boost your self-worth. This can be of particular benefit to those of us with attachment styles characterized by low self-esteem.

Making – and Keeping – Friends

Meeting New People

So we understand the value of making new friends. But, as we've discussed, meeting new people is not the easiest thing to do, particularly when our modern-day lives are so busy.

Here are a few ways to go about meeting people and forging new friendships:

- Volunteer at your local charity, or for a cause you are passionate about.

- Join a club or take a class. This will put you in contact with many people who share your interests.

- Attend book signing, lecture, gallery, recital and other event in your community in which you might meet people with similar interests.

- Go to a sporting event. While it can be daunting being in a crowd on your own, bonding over shared loved of your sports team can be a great way to meet new people. If you don't feel comfortable attending the match on your own, what about going to watch the game in a bar? You'll have the same opportunity to connect with others, but on a much smaller scale.

- Turn off your phone. No matter where you are, it is difficult to meet new people if you are wearing headphones, or if your head is buried in your smartphone. Put down the phone and engage with the world – and the people – around you.

Strengthening Existing Acquaintances

Making new friends does not necessarily have to mean meeting new people. In many cases, making new friends can be a matter of simply strengthening your existing acquaintances. Here are a few ideas for turning acquaintances into friends:

- Break the ice by inviting a colleague or neighbor out for coffee or a drink.
- Track down old friends on social media and rekindle the friendship by inviting them to meet in person.
- Connect with your college alumni.

Dealing With Fear of Rejection

Just like when you're in the dating pool, making new friends means putting yourself out there and opening yourself up to rejection. This can be scary, particularly for those who suffer from an anxious preoccupied attachment style. In Chapter Ten we will be looking at ways of addressing and healing our attachment issues in order to deal with rejection, among other things. But here are few other key points to keep in mind if you find yourself being rejected by someone you had hoped to build a friendship with:

- If someone rejects your invitation, remember it does not necessarily mean they are rejecting you as a person. Everyone has their own busy life, of which we likely know very little about. Their refusal may just be because they are busy or distracted.

- Similarly, if someone rejects you, it does not mean you are inherently unlikeable, or unworthy of friendship. It's possible that the person just misunderstood you, or are having a bad day. Or perhaps their behavior is more to do with their own insecurities and attachment issues.

- Keep rejection in perspective. Instead of beating yourself up over it, see it as a learning experience – and one that strengthens you, allowing to learn for next time and become a stronger person.

Cultivating Long-Lasting Friendships

What Makes a Good Friend?

Knowing what we look for in a friend can go a long way towards helping us build long-lasting friendships. It reduces the potential for conflict and drama, and helps us manage any problems that may arise due to our attachment issues.

Firstly, take some time to determine what makes a good friend in your opinion. Perhaps they are those who:

- Show genuine interest in you and your life
- Are always there for you in times of need
- Don't judge you, even when you make mistakes
- Never deliberately hurt your feelings
- Never put you down
- You enjoy their company
- Are loyal and trustworthy

- You can laugh and cry with
- Will tell you the truth, even when it is hard to hear
- Will always listen
- You feel comfortable sharing your emotions with

Ask yourself how you feel when you're around a particular person. Does spending time with them make you feel better or worse? Are you yourself when you're around this person, or do you put on a façade, uncomfortable of revealing your true self? Does this person treat you with respect? Do you feel as though this is a person you can trust? (Incidentally, these are all excellent questions to ask yourself when navigating early romantic relationships too.)

How to be a good friend

The best way of maintaining lasting friendships, of course, is to be a good friend yourself. Think back to the characteristics that you determined make a good friend, and ensure you are exhibiting these traits in your own relationships.

Here are just a few of the ways you can work towards being a good friend towards those you care about:

- Listen: If a friend is sharing his or her problems with you, ensure you engage in active listening; concentrate, do your best to retain information and offer a well-thought-out response. Ask questions. Do your best to see the situation from your friend's point of view. If you don't have all the answers, don't worry. Likely, your friend is not coming to you for a solution to their problem, they just need a sympathetic ear on which to unload. This can be a particularly difficult thing to do if you suffer from an avoidant attachment style, which is characterised by a lack of empathy.
- Ask What You Can Do to Help: If your friend is facing a difficult situation, don't wait for them to ask for ask help. Instead,

actively ask them what they need and what you can do to help. This will lead them to reciprocate when you find yourself in a challenging situation.

- Show physical affection: This can be another big challenge for those with avoidant attachment styles. But hugging your friends is a great way to show you care, and the physical contact increases the bond between you. All humans need physical contact with others in order to survive. An act as simple as a hug can prevent both you and your friend from feeling alone.

- Keep in Touch: Keeping in touch with our friends can be difficult at times, especially for those of us with large friendship circles and social networks. But taking time out of your busy schedule to connect with a friend is a great way to maintain closeness and strength in the friendship. It doesn't need to be a long-winded phone call. If you are short on time, send a short text or message on social media, just to let your friend know you are thinking of them.

- Share Your Feelings: Tell your friends what they mean to you. Just as in romantic relationships, your friends can't be expected to know how you feel if you have not told them. This is especially true for friends with anxious preoccupied personalities. This kind of honesty and openness goes a long way towards building lasting friendships. And for those of you who feel uncomfortable opening up and sharing your feelings, remember that the more you do it, the easier it will get.

CHAPTER TEN: HOW TO HEAL
ATTACHMENT WOUNDS

As we have learned throughout this book, without intervention, those of us with an insecure attachment style will go on to re-live the negative experiences of their childhood, resulting in strained, stressful and painful experiences throughout their life. These issues can manifest in romantic relationships, friendships, relationships with family and colleagues, as well as the way we relate to ourselves.

But, deep-seated as those these attachment wounds may be, they are able to be healed. It is important to believe that secure attachment is possible for everyone. There are many ways in which attachment trauma can be healed, and in this chapter we will address both self-healing methods and some of the many methods that may be used when working with a therapist.

Self-Directed Healing

Healing becomes possible when we focus on rewiring our brain and creating new experiences of positive emotional connection. In time, these new thought processes will replace the old behavioural patterns that were brought about by our negative childhood experiences.

Let's take a look at some of the ways you can work at healing your attachment wounds:

Allow Yourself to Grieve

The healing process is a process of grieving. When you become aware of the incidents and situations that caused your attachment issues to form, it is likely that you will feel some degree of loss and sadness. This grief will come about with the realization that you suffered neglect as a child, or from the absence of any real emotional connection to your primary caregiver.

Accepting the need for new patterns and getting rid of the old is a grief process. You are mourning both what did happen, and also the safe, secure relationships that *did not* happen. Allow yourself to feel and accept this pain, before releasing it and moving on.

Make Sense of Our Story

If we can understand exactly what the narrative is that is driving our attachment issues, it helps us to see how it is affecting us in our adult lives. It may also make us aware that we are passing down the same narrative and issues to our own children.

These issues may be things we usually associate with the word "trauma" such as bereavement, abuse or other life-threatening situations. But the reality is that most of us carry around the effects of smaller "traumas" – many of which are unconscious. These can be things like dealing with a parent who was always at work, or was too busy dealing with their own emotional issues to really be present when in our company. This trauma could be related to one particular moment, or a series of incidents that took place over time and cumulatively resulted in your attachment style.

The issues that brought about our trauma may not always be obvious, as any emotional abuse we suffered as a child may not be immediately clear. For example, we may have had an outwardly loving and participatory parent who, despite their best intentions, did not offer any true emotional connection or engagement. Often due to their own attachment issues, this parent may have been either available, or been unwilling to really understand the workings of their child's mind. This kind of chronic emotional absence can have the same negative effect on a child as more obvious emotional abuse.

By facing and understanding our past traumas, we can change our attachment patterns; in time altering the course of our relationships and our, ultimately, our lives.

Find a Partner with a Secure Attachment Style

As we have seen in previous chapters, partners with secure attachment styles can be invaluable resources in assisting their loved ones to break out of their negative attachment patterns. Developing a secure relationship with someone who already exhibits a secure attachment style can help increase our self-worth and sense of security, as our new partnership forms an active model for how successful relationships operate. Possibly, those of us with insecure attachment styles have never been part of a secure relationship before, owing to the constant recreation of the negative patterns experienced in childhood.

But entering a healing relationship with a securely attached partner can be a frightening experience for many people suffering from insecure attachment styles. Many insecures, particularly those with an avoidant attachment style struggle to open up and connect with others, and the idea that a partner may seek emotional intimacy can be overwhelming.

Some people with insecure attachment styles may believe it is necessary to handle all their issues themselves and never ask for help. Others may believe that sharing their problems is futile, as no one could possibly understand what they are going through. Sharing and opening up might also make them feel weak. And for those with dismissive avoidant or fearful avoidant attachment styles, being alone might be the only thing that makes them feel safe.

But for those of you struggling to connect with a secure partner, understand that cultivating a healthy relationship has the power to repair even the most deep-seated of emotional wounds.

Choose a life of connection; not just with your significant other, but in all relationship aspects. Shift your focus about how you define relationships and realise that all relationships are important. Counter the patterns of disconnect you have previously experienced by actively inviting connection into your life.

Make a plan to live a life of connection and value all your relationships. Remember, as humans, we need connection to survive. Surrounding us with those we care about gives us security, comfort, inspiration, clarity and grounding.

Question Your Core Beliefs About Yourself

Remember those who caused your attachment issues had their own problems. These may have come in the form of addiction, preoccupation, work issues, their own dramas, or marriage issues. Very rarely, if ever, was their behaviour a direct reflection on you.

Nonetheless, our attachment issues create a set of negative core beliefs we have about ourselves. We tell ourselves stories about what happened, and draw our own, often unconscious conclusions. For example, "Dad was always at work, therefore I don't matter." Or "Mom never real listened to me, so I must be unlovable." We personalise the events that took place during our childhood and develop deep-seated core beliefs about ourselves that effect our adult life.

These negative beliefs form obstacles when it comes to building relationships. How can we have a successful relationship when we are lugging around the belief that we are unlovable and do not deserve to be in a relationship? How can we have a successful relationship when we don't believe we are good enough, or don't' believe that we matter?

Successfully healing our attachment wounds requires us to really confront our core beliefs and examine just what it is we feel about ourselves. Most often, these beliefs leave us to have a diminished sense of self-worth.

Confront the Romantic Narrative

As we touched in Chapter Seven, our culture is constantly presenting us with an ideal of what a romantic relationship should look like. We've all seen and heard this story countless times – a couple falls in love at first sight, and they are deliriously happy. They get to know each other more which leads them to discover that they are each other's soulmate. And of course, they live happily ever after.

But as even those of us with the most secure attachment styles know, the reality of being in a relationship is often far removed from this ideal. Comparing our relationships to this fantasy ideal is unrealistic, immature and unhealthy, particularly for those of us struggling with negative attachment issues.

In the same way that we must identify and question our core beliefs about ourselves, healing attachment trauma requires us to look at our beliefs regarding what a relationship should look like. As yourself how you believe couples "should" meet, interact, grow, share passion and otherwise relate. Then ask yourself where this belief has come from. Is it based on the fantasy of the ideal relationship the media presents us on a regular basis?

If we continue to compare our relationships to the fantasy romantic narrative, we are setting ourselves up for disappointment, as real-life partners will never compare to this ideal.

Strengthen our Self-Compassion

This point ties into the previous two, in which we questioned our core beliefs and our beliefs about the world around us. It calls on us to actively cultivate a greater sense of kindness to ourselves. By doing this, we are not only undoing any negative beliefs we might have about our self-worth, but we are replacing these damaging beliefs with a kinder inner dialogue.

By doing this, we will be able to more easily set boundaries, along with raising our standards and expectations in relationships of all kinds.

A big part of this is teaching ourselves not to accept anything less than true connection. This can be very difficult for those of us with anxious attachment styles, who have grown up accepting whatever miserable scraps of connection we can manage. People with attachment issues have taught themselves to live with emotionally unavailable, or emotionally demanding partners, often out of the fear that they will never find anyone better. They stay in damaging relationships, or with partners they don't feel connected to, believing that a flawed relationship is better than no relationship at all.

To break out of this pattern, allow yourself to question your relationships and the quality of the love and connection you are receiving. Realign your core belief to accept that you are worthy of true love and connection.

Pay Attention to Your Physical Body

Like all other psychological issues, attachment trauma can manifest itself in our physical body. In Chapter One, we discussed some of the physical effects of attachment issues, from an increased fight of flight response, to the altering of our genes as infants, which can cause health issues in later life. We have also discussed the correlation between healthy familial relationships and health and later life, and seen how supressing our feelings can manifest as physical symptoms such as stomach pains.

When you are working at healing your attachment injuries, it is important to pay attention to the way your physical body is feeling. The link between our mind and our body is undeniable, so observing the way you physically respond to these healing activities can provide you with a good gauge as to their effectiveness.

Pay attention to any pain or discomfort you are feeling within your body and any areas in which you might be carrying stress or tension.

Listen to your body as you go through the above healing exercises and notice the appearance or disappearance of any pain or discomfort.

Working With a Therapist

While self-directed healing can produce amazing results, sometimes our attachment wounds are simply too deep or too complex for us to manage on our own. This is when it becomes important to enlist the help of a licenced therapist.

A productive therapy session will help clients identify different parts of themselves that they may not have been aware of. A trained therapist will help you understand that your perceived strengths are often covers for underlying hurt and trauma and understand how these issues relate to your everyday behaviour and tendencies.

Therapy can help us connect to our inner child – that often-scared part of us that needs emotional connection, love and support. Therapy can teach us to offer kindness and compassion to this inner child, instead of responding to our own perceived failures with negative self-talk.

Therapy can also help us to identify the opportunities for secure attachment that exist all around us. In all likelihood we have a network of caring friends or family – no matter how big or small – who are eager and willing to offer support when necessary. Remember, our survival depends on staying in close contact with those we love. Even the most independent of humans cannot survive alone.

While therapy sessions may incorporate many of the self-healing techniques we have discussed, there are also a number of different techniques and processes therapists may use in order to get to the root of your attachment injuries.

Let's take a look:

Psychoanalysis Therapy

Psychoanalysis aims to release repressed emotions and experiences, in other words, to make us aware of previous unconscious memories. Although there is some variety in technique from therapist to therapist, this generally involves the patient lying on a couch, unable to see the therapist. They will be asked questions about their day-to-day thoughts and conflicts. This then leads the therapist to ask more probing and confronting questions, along with the analysis of dreams and fantasies, with the ultimate intent of uncovering hidden memories from early life.

Cognitive Behavioural Therapy

Unlike psychoanalysis, cognitive behavioural therapy, or CBT, does not aim to take the patient back in time. Instead, it helps you make sense of what is going on in your head, and provides techniques for dealing with seemingly irrational fears and emotions. This is done through the analysis of five different areas in your life; situations, thoughts, emotions, physical feelings and actions, all of which are intrinsically connected. Through in-depth discussion, therapists will help patients identify the core beliefs at the root of their problems and help them replace their damaging inner dialogue with more positive thoughts, implementing behaviors that support these new beliefs.

The Hoffman Process

The Hoffman process, created by Bob Hoffman in 1967, is a guided process of group therapy that aims to uncover the root causes of our attachment issues and injuries. Over an intense week-long retreat, the process teaches participants to trace the root of their negative behavioural patterns, and dissolve their damaging beliefs. The process combines a number of techniques, including psychoanalysis and CBT. Participants also engage in journaling, guided meditation and visualization, with the end goal of cultivating compassion for both themselves, their parents and others in their lives.

Hypnotherapy

Hypnosis can be a useful technique for uncovering hidden memories and discovering the root cause of our emotional issues. By entering a hypnotic state, patients are more likely to obtain access to deeply buried memories and uncover the underlying causes, or causes, of their attachment issues.

How to Find the Right Therapist

With so many therapists out there, finding the right one for you can seem like a daunting task. In a way, it's a bit like dating – finding someone with whom you resonate, and who you feel truly understands you. While it can be time consuming to find the right therapist, it is well worth putting in the time. Studies have proven that a good relationship with a therapist or counsellor can cause the brain to literally rewire itself, leading to real, long-lasting positive changes. So here are a few things to keep in mind when you're trawling through a seemingly endless list of available therapists:

- Start by narrowing down the list. This can be as simple as filtering out those who are not in your vicinity. By taking this small step, it can make the process immediately feel more manageable.
- Read through your list and get an instinctive feeling about each therapist. Learn a little about each of the professionals on your list – their background, their professional views, their life experiences. Rule out any with whom you don't feel as though you resonate, or could connect with.
- Develop a vague idea of the approach you want. Do you want to quickly remove the symptoms of your attachment wounds? Or do you want to really understand the causes at the root of your injuries by accessing long-buried memories?

- With your goal in mind, take some time to research a few of the different approaches to healing attachment wounds. Which of these approaches do you feel is right for you?

- Ultimately, successful therapy relies on a strong relationship between the patient and therapist. Many therapists offer a free initial consultation phone call, so be sure to take advantage of this. Even if, after this, you feel as though you have found the right person to help you work through your issues, you may like to begin with just one or two sessions, to really ensure you have a strong connection with the person you are working with. After all, this is a relationship that has the power to greatly change your life for the better.

CONCLUSION

As we have come to see throughout the course of this book, the issues caused by our attachment style begin very early in life, in the formative years before we can even properly communicate. Even those of us with the most loving of parents can experience attachment issues to some degree.

If you have not done so already, take some time to really analyse your behavioural and thought patterns, particularly in the field of relationships. Ask yourself the questions in Chapter Three, and examine the love personalities presented in Chapter Four. Can you see yourself in any of these attachment styles and personalities?

It is important to remember too, that even those of us with a primarily secure attachment style can exhibits anxious or avoidant tendencies at times. While the manifestations of these attachment styles may not be as profound as for someone with attachment issues, they can still present obstacles on the road to happy relationships. Even the mildest of manifestations can be solved by addressing the underlying issues and implementing the techniques discussed in Chapter Ten.

Above all, remember that, no matter how many years you have been carrying around your attachment wounds, they are always able to be healed. While the process can be uncomfortable and even painful at times, understand that releasing your attachment issues is among the most valuable things you can do for yourself. By doing so, you will open the door to a greater sense of self-worth, valuable friendships, strong familial ties and a long-lasting and loving romantic relationships. It is always possible to make changes, and doing so can allow you to finally find the happiness, love and security you have been seeking for so long.